The Urge Overtakes Me and I Must Write

Shelia Lirette

Copyright © 2016 Shelia Lirette

All rights reserved.

ISBN: 153739570X
ISBN-13: 978-1537395708

DEDICATION

THIS BOOK IS DEDICATED TO ALL THOSE
WHO FEEL THE NEED TO WRITE THEIR
THOUGHTS, THEIR EMOTIONS, THEIR LIFE.
ENJOY AND WRITE ON,
MY FRIEND.

With the New Day Comes New Strength and New Thoughts. Eleanor Roosevelt

Don't walk in front of me!
I may not follow. Albert Camus

Problems are Not Stop Signs,
They are Guidelines. Robert H. Schuller

I Am So Clever That Sometimes I Don't Understand a Single Word of What I Am Saying. - Oscar Wilde

Accept the challenges so that you can feel the exhilaration of victory. George S. Patton

Doodle Your Dreams

Outside of a Dog, a Book is Man's Best Friend.
Inside of a Dog It's Too Dark to Read. - Groucho Marx

Live Well! Take Time to Enjoy Life!

Keep smiling, because life's a beautiful thing and there's so much to smile about.   Marilyn Monroe

You may say I'm a dreamer, but I'm not the only one.
I hope someday you'll join us.
And the world will live as one. John Lennon

Doodly Doodly Dum

**It is impossible to live
without failing at something.**
J.K. Rowling

Imagination Encircles the World.
Albert Einstein

It's Okay to Have a Good Day - Really! Unknown

> Don't watch the clock;
> do what it does. Keep going.
> Sam Levenson

Everything Has Its Beauty,
But Not Everyone Sees It. - Andy Warhol

To be yourself in a world that is
constantly trying to make you something
else is the greatest accomplishment. Ralph Waldo Emerson

> Some people never go crazy. What truly horrible lives they must lead. Charles Bukowski

Failure will never overtake me if my determination to succeed is strong enough. Og Mandino

Sing like there's nobody listening
William W. Purkey

Draw Your Dreams

> Love looks not with
> the eyes, but with the mind,
> And therefore is winged Cupid
> painted blind.   William Shakespeare

You only live once,
but if you do it right,
once is enough. Mae West

The Secret of Getting Ahead
is Getting Started. Mark Twain

Anyone Who Has Never Made a Mistake has Never Tried Anything New.   Albert Einstein

Imperfection is beauty, madness is genius and it's better to be absolutely ridiculous than absolutely boring. Marilyn Monroe

> All that is gold does not glitter,
> Not all those who wander are lost
> J.R.R. Tolkien

> The truth is, everyone is going to hurt you. You just got to find the ones worth suffering for. Bob Marley

I Begin With An Idea and Then It
Becomes Something Else. - Pablo Picasso

Failure Will Never Overtake Me If My Determination to Succeed is Strong Enough. Og Mandino

> Twenty years from now you will be more disappointed by the things that you didn't do than by the ones you did do. H. Jackson Brown Jr.

The Way to Get Started is to Quit
Talking and Begin Doing. Walt Disney

Don't Be Afraid to Dream!

Start Where You Are. Use What You Have.
Do What You Can. Arthur Ashe

> You know you're in love when you can't fall asleep because reality is finally better than your dreams. Dr. Seuss

> When one door of happiness closes, another opens; but often we look so long at the closed door that we do not see the one which has been opened for us. Helen Keller

> You know you're in love when you can't fall asleep because reality is finally better than your dreams. Dr. Seuss

Stop building other's dreams, start building yours right now. John Rampton

Doodle Time

Catch the trade winds in your sails.
Explore. Dream. Discover.
H. Jackson Brown Jr.

You are never too old to set another goal or to dream a new dream. C. S. Lewis

> Who are you to judge the life I live?
> I know I'm not perfect and I don't
> live to be but before you start pointing fingers
> ... make sure you hands are clean! Bob Marley

Today you are You,
that is truer than true.
Dr. Seuss

Awesomeness!

I'm not afraid of death;
I just don't want to be there
when it happens. Woody Allen

This life is what you make it.
No matter what, you're going to
mess up sometimes, it's a universal
truth. Marilyn Monroe

> Throw off the bowlines. Sail away from the safe harbor. Catch the trade winds in your sails. H. Jackson Brown Jr.

Don't walk behind me! I may not lead.
Albert Camus

Always, Always Believe in Yourself,
Because if You Don't,
Then Who Will, Sweetie - Marilyn Monroe

Good, better, best.
Never let it rest, 'Til your
good is better and your better
is best. St. Jerome

Doodle Dreaming

It Is Never Too Late To Be What
You Might Have Been. - George Eliot

With the New Day Comes New Strength and New Thoughts. Eleanor Roosevelt

The way to get started
is to quit talking and begin
doing. Walt Disney

With the New Day Comes New Strength and New Thoughts. Eleanor Roosevelt

In order to succeed,
we must first believe that
we can. Nikos Kazantzakis

Walk beside me; just be my friend.
Albert Camus

I am good, but not an angel.
I do sin, but I am not the devil. I
am just a small girl in a big world trying
to find someone to love.   Marilyn Monroe

Keep your face to the
sunshine and you cannot
see a shadow. Helen Keller

Doodle On

One good thing about
music, when it hits you,
you feel no pain. Bob Marley

> Always do your best. What you plant now, you will harvest later. Og Mandino

Sometimes good things fall apart
so better things can fall together. Marilyn Monroe

The only way out of
the labyrinth of suffering
is to forgive. John Green

Don't walk in front of me!
I may not follow. Albert Camus

Outside of a Dog, a Book is Man's Best Friend.
Inside of a Dog It's Too Dark to Read. - Groucho Marx

> I am enough of an artist to draw
> freely upon my imagination. Imagination
> is more important than knowledge. Knowledge
> is limited. Imagination encircles
> the world. Albert Einstein

Keep Your Eyes on the Stars, and Your Feet on the Ground. Theodore Roosevelt

Yesterday is history,
tomorrow is a mystery,
today is a gift of God,
which is why we call it the present. Bil Keane

It matters not what someone is born, but what they grow to be. J.K. Rowling

In Three Words I Can Sum Up Everything
I've Learned About Life: It Goes On. - Robert Frost

Dream Big...Set Goals...
Take Action
Unknown

A Creative Man is Motivated by the Desire to Achieve,
Not by the Desire to Beat Others. Ayn Rand

I am a common man with
common thoughts and I've led
a common life.   Nicholas Sparks

Draw Your Dreams

There are only two ways to live your life. One is as though nothing is a miracle. The other is as though everything is a miracle. Albert Einstein

I Have Not Failed. I've Just Found 10,000 Ways That Won't Work - Thomas A. Edison

Outside of a Dog, a Book is Man's Best Friend.
Inside of a Dog It's Too Dark to Read. - Groucho Marx

It is better to remain silent at the
risk of being thought a fool, than to
talk and remove all doubt of it. Maurice Switzer

**Problems are Not Stop Signs,
They are Guidelines.** Robert H. Schuller

ABOUT THE AUTHOR

As a Florida Native, Shelia enjoys all things "beachy" and visits several beaches each year.

In fact, the photographs behind the lines in the journal are pictures she took at Lover's Key Beach which is located around Bonita Beach FL.

She has written over twenty articles, a children's book, An Adventure on Spook Hill, and at least a couple of illustrated journals.

She has been self-employed for over ten years and is an accomplished artist and entrepreneur. She continues to write, create and explore new locations.

www.ingramcontent.com/pod-product-compliance
Lightning Source LLC
Chambersburg PA
CBHW060408190526
45169CB00002B/812